MODERN ROMANTIC WEDDINGS

MODERN
ROMANTIC
WEDDINGS

MAGGIE LORD

GIBBS SMITH
TO ENRICH AND INSPIRE HUMANKIND

First Edition

23 22 21 20 19   5 4 3 2 1

Published by
Gibbs Smith
P.O. Box 667
Layton, Utah 84041

1.800.835.4993 orders
www.gibbs-smith.com

Designed by Tracy Sunrize Johnson
Printed and bound in China

Gibbs Smith books are printed on either recy-cled, 100% post-consumer waste, FSC-certified papers or on paper produced from sustainable PEFC-certified forest/controlled wood source. Learn more at www.pefc.org.

Library of Congress Cataloging-in-Publication Data

Names: Lord, Maggie, author.
Title: Modern romantic weddings / Maggie Lord.
Description: First edition. | Layton, Utah : Gibbs Smith, [2019]
Identifiers: LCCN 2018060858 | ISBN 9781423650607 (jacketless hardcover)
Subjects: LCSH: Weddings--United States--Planning.
Classification: LCC HQ745 .L6699 2019 | DDC 392.5--dc23
LC record available at https://lccn.loc.gov/2018060858

For my boys, Jack, Charlie & William,
who have misbehaved at several weddings!

CONTENTS

INTRODUCTION

A WEDDING IS A CELEBRATION: a celebration of love, family, friends, and the start of something new and wonderful. No matter the style, the location, or the budget, everyone wants their wedding to be filled with beauty and romance. This book is designed to help inspire and guide you as you plan your own modern romantic wedding. As you plan this special day remember to enjoy the process and to release yourself from the stress that can come with hosting such a large event. My hope for anyone planning a wedding is to lose yourself in the dreamy images you fantasize about and to forget about things you don't have control over, like the weather or why your cousin's girlfriend showed up without RSVPing.

In 2008, I founded RusticWeddingChic.com because I was completely and utterly obsessed with weddings and the wedding planning process, and I was in the middle of planning my own rustic chic wedding. When I was in this planning process back in 2008 it was a different landscape than today—there was no Pinterest, no Instagram and most of my wedding ideas were found in wedding magazines. It was my goal to create an online wedding resource that allowed readers to be inspired and find information on how to plan their dream day. After sharing ten years' worth of real weddings, DIY projects, budget saving tricks, and wedding inspiration I am so pleased to bring my information off-line and share my fourth book focused on weddings. My hope for you is to travel away to someplace beautiful in your mind as you page through this book while sipping a warm cup of coffee or a chilled glass of bubbly.

xoxo,
Maggie

WEDDING PLANNING 101

After the question has been popped, and you have said "yes," the realization that you actually need to plan a wedding sets in. For many, this can seem like an overwhelming process. To set you on your way to stress-free planning, Wedding Planning 101 helps break down everything you need to know.

After you have celebrated, popped champagne, and told all your closest friends and family, it is important to put some ideas on paper. Start with *where* you want to get married, *when* you want to get married, and the *number of guests* you would like to host.

A fun way to start this process is to have both you and your partner answer these questions separately from each other and then compare your responses. You might find that you both have a similar, if not the same, idea for a location, date, and number of guests.

THE WEDDING DATE

The wedding date may *seem* easy to determine between the two of you, but you would be surprised how many date and location changes you might have to go through once you loop close family and friends into the mix. Begin with a few weekends in mind. Oftentimes you'll finalize your wedding date based on the availability of your ideal venue, the availability of everyone in your wedding party, or both.

THE WEDDING LOCATION

Selecting your wedding location is one of the largest tasks you need to take on when planning your dream day—many of the other wedding details will fall into place after you have decided on a location and a venue. The wedding location and the wedding venue are actually two different decisions that need to be made. The location of the wedding is the state, town, or city in which your wedding will take place. The venue is the physical location where the wedding will be held. When researching, and later selecting, your wedding location it is important to have an idea of the type of event you want to host. Will your wedding require travel for most guests? Will the wedding be held in one of your hometowns, or will it be hosted where you currently live as a couple? These are questions that need to be asked *before* moving on to venue options. If you are hoping for an outdoor wedding ceremony and reception, consider a venue that can provide an indoor option if the weather is less than optimal on your wedding day. Many couples are faced with hosting their ceremony at one venue and their reception at a neighboring location. If you think your wedding will fall into this category, make sure to plan for transportation between the two spots.

If you are hosting your ceremony at a place of worship, you'll need to coordinate the date with an opening there and at your reception venue, so the earlier you can start to plan your dates, the better. Also, some places of worship request specific paperwork or even pre-marriage classes in addition to the marriage licences, so you will need to know what is required of you ahead of time and plan for that as well.

A wedding where the majority of the guests will have to travel no matter the location is a destination wedding. For example, I planned my own wedding in a small Midwestern town where my family has a summer house. All of our guests needed to travel from out of town, so allowing extra time for guests to plan for details, like how to get there and where to stay, was key. If this is the case for you, get those save-the-dates out to your guests at least nine months before your wedding; if international travel is involved, twelve months is preferred.

VENUE IDEAS

Small inns and bed & breakfasts

Historical sites and famous houses

Museums and art galleries

College clubs and university venues

Gardens and arboretums

Retail spaces like bookstores or antiques stores

Large resorts

Farms and barns

Vineyards and breweries

Restaurants

Beach clubs

State Parks

Houses and estates for rent via online sites such as Airbnb or VRBO

How do we determine how formal (or informal) the ceremony and reception should be?

You might have been dreaming of a black tie event and your fiancé might be thinking more along the lines of a simple backyard affair. Make sure you are on the same page when it comes to how formal you would like your wedding day to be. The formality will impact the type of venues, services, and vendors you select. There are no rules to follow about how formal or informal a wedding should be, even given the venue you select. You as the couple get to create your own rules and set the tone for how formal or informal you want the day to be. Many couples choose to host a formal event in an interesting, less traditionally formal location (such as a garden or lakeside resort). On the flip side, some couples host an informal event at a tented reception on the grounds of an estate. The power you have as the wedding couple allows you to decide on the formality of the event and to create a vibe all your own.

MAGGIE'S TIP: *Many clubs and certain institutions require jackets for men and could prohibit such clothing as jeans, sneakers, or sandals so be sure to research these specifics.*

THE NUMBER OF GUESTS

The number of guests you want to have at your wedding is as personal a choice as what style of dress you want to wear. Many times the venue will influence the guest count based on the number of people it can accommodate. If you want to have your wedding on a beach, this space allows you to create a guest list count as high as you choose since the space is unlimited; if you are considering a venue like a barn or dining room, the number of guests you can invite will go down. Couples get very creative when working on how they can achieve their guest list number. Many couples decide they will eliminate inviting coworkers (which often makes the guest list spike) or they might decide that not every guest will be given an automatic plus-one for the event.

If your parents would like to invite friends of theirs, and your budget and venue allows for that, a good rule of thumb many couples work with is to assign a set number of guests each set of parents can invite and a separate number of guests for the bride and groom to invite. This will allow each family to share in the big day with the people who are important to them but also allows the couple to feel as if they get to control the number of guests in total.

You might have a rough number in your head but there is a good chance that number will change once you get the list of who you and your partner's family would like to invite. It is also good to at least have a rough ideas of how many guests you might invite when looking at venues so you know if your picture-perfect venue can accommodate your guest list.

Whether or not children will be invited to the wedding is a question really only you and your partner can answer because it is a very personal choice. Some couples decide that they would like to have a more adult wedding and that means not inviting children. Others simply feel having the children of their guests present would create budget issues, as the guest list could grow considerably. Some couples include only the children who are in the wedding party and those of close family members, and that works too. If you are not set on having an adults-only wedding you might find that having children at the wedding adds an element of fun. Children and young adults are usually willing to dance and often get the party started! Whatever you decide to do, make sure you communicate your wishes to your guests clearly so there are no misunderstandings.

MAGGIE'S TIP: *Create a separate kids' area stocked with coloring options, bubbles, lawn games, or even Lego-like building toys at the reception. This will ensure even your littlest guests (and their parents) are happy.*

WEDDING PARTY

Not everyone decides to enlist a bridal party. Or they choose to limit their
wedding party to one or two people. Check with your fiancé to see what they
are thinking, and then create a list of who (if anyone) will be in your wedding
party. Today couples are creating wedding parties to fit their personal style,
so feel free to have a large or small wedding party and feel free to break some
"rules" and have special people—not just bridesmaids and groomsmen—in
your party.

Don't worry about details like an uneven number of bridesmaids and groomsmen. It is more about *who* you want to be part of this special crew on your wedding day than whether the numbers are even. Many couples today select the people most special to them without expecting them to play the traditional gender role of bridesmaid or groomsman. If you want to have your male best friend as your man of honor instead of a maid of honor, go for it! If your groom wants his two sisters to be his groomswomen, that works too. Tailoring your wedding party to spotlight the special people in your lives as a couple is what is important.

There is an opportunity to have people in your wedding party outside of bridesmaids and groomsmen as well, which means assigning roles (if you choose) such as flower girls, ring bearers, or even ushers. Often times these specific titles are perfect for family members or friends you want to highlight, but whose roles don't require a great deal of responsibility.

One way to involve a special family member or friend is to ask them to be the officiant of the wedding. It does not take much to gain the power to officiate a wedding service (just an application and small fee, submitted online) and this can often be the perfect duty for someone who means a great deal to you and your fiancé.

MAGGIE'S TIP: *Many couples want their dog to be part of the ceremony. This is super cute, but make sure to ask one specific person to be in charge of your four-legged friend before, during, and after the ceremony so you don't have any panic moments!*

BUDGET

Weddings get expensive (and quickly!) so creating a budget is not only helpful but necessary. Most likely, your wedding will be the largest party you have ever thrown so planning how and where you will spend your money is key. There are endless amounts of resources online including spreadsheets, phone apps, and computer software to help you plan, save, and spend on your wedding day—take advantage of them. No matter the budget you have available to you, your dream wedding can be achieved with a clear vision for the day and strategic planning. Many couples will save in one area in order to splurge in another, or couples will delete items that don't apply to their specific wedding style or theme. If you are working with a limited budget consider pushing your wedding date more than twelve months after your engagement. More time to plan allows for more time to build up wedding savings and to not be rushed into any decisions.

MAGGIE'S TIP: *Ask guests to RSVP online rather than including a return envelope and postage in your invitation.*

Perhaps one of the most difficult topics in wedding planning is *how* you will be paying for the wedding. If you think you and your partner will be receiving assistance from parents or family members, make sure you have a conversation early on in the process. You'll need a firm dollar amount to work with when budgeting. If one or more people are helping you foot the bill, ask if they are going to be writing you a check (allowing you and your partner to decide how and where to spend the money) or if they will be paying for specific wedding items themselves (and want the invoices forwarded to them).

Is there an easy to way to trim my budget?

The quickest way to run up a wedding budget is with the number of guests. The more people you will be hosting, the more tables, chairs, food, drink, and space you'll be needing. If you cut down the number of guests you invite, your budget will have some room to breathe. Other ways to trim expenses can actually result in a more unique wedding, so don't be afraid to skip something traditional in favor of something you truly love (such as skipping the formal cake and going with donuts from your favorite bakery).

SIMPLE WAYS TO SAVE MONEY

Plan a Friday night wedding

Host your wedding in the morning or early afternoon

Have a dance-free wedding and only play music for ambiance: skipping the band or DJ means saving thousands; lovely background music can be achieved with your computer or phone

Serve two signature cocktails and don't offer a full bar, or just serve wine and beer

Keep your wedding party to just one or two on each side: the fewer people in your wedding party, the less you need to spend on bouquets, transportation, and details like hair and makeup

Host the ceremony and reception at one location so you can eliminate paying for transportation

Limit your guest list to family and just a set number of "outsiders"

Use email or send postcards as save-the-dates

Avoid costly favors for guests, offering up your mother-in-law's beloved caramels or a bundle of herbs from your garden instead

Skip the bouquets and opt to carry a single flower or nothing at all

Consider buying a pre-owned wedding gown or shop for a white gown that is not technically a wedding dress

Select a venue where all rentals (tables and chairs) are included

Skip the traditional catering and work with food trucks or use an alternative-style catering company

Limit the photographer's hours: opt for five hours of coverage and not a pricier option like ten hours

Create one wedding menu that can be displayed and skip the printing costs for individual menus at each place setting

Rent houses for the wedding party and skip the hotels

Limit your plus-ones to guests who are over college age

Is it okay to skip some of the classic wedding traditions?

Different wedding traditions are special to people for different reasons. Take a moment to examine what traditions speak to you and your fiancé and which ones do not. Do you love the idea of wearing white or are you excited to rock a dress in a bold color? Would you like to have bridesmaids (or special people) standing next to you as you say "I do" or would you rather it just be you and your partner? Is a sit-down dinner right for your style of wedding or should you have a cocktail party instead? Do you want to toss your bouquet or conclude the evening in a different way?

Keep in mind, what *you* may not consider an important tradition might be important to your partner, your mom, your grandmother, or soon-to-be mother-in-law. Make sure you fill them in on what traditions you want to keep and what you want to omit.

"We agonized over which wedding traditions we could forego and which ones we needed to keep so our families wouldn't feel like they "missed out." But then we realized, it's just a big party. Have fun with it. If you're happy, your family will be happy."

—Kerry (Bride)

5 TRADITIONS THAT ARE
OKAY TO SKIP

1. Bridal party

Having a bridal party is not for everyone. In fact, not having one can simplify lots of details about your big day and save on your budget. There is no rule that says you need to have bridesmaids, groomsmen, or special people standing up with you!

2. First dance

Not everyone is comfortable dancing in front of a big crowd and more recently I have seen couples cut out the traditional first dance; instead they ask their entertainment to simply welcome everyone to the dance floor to start the party.

3. Cake cutting

Many times cutting the cake is done on the side and is just for pictures, but you can skip this part of the evening and have your catering crew just serve the cake or the sweet treats to your guests.

4. Bouquet toss

I have to be honest, I hardly ever see this tradition anymore. As the night goes on, brides don't want to spend time gathering all of the single women together to toss the bouquet, You shouldn't feel bad about tossing this tradition either.

5. Speeches

After a simple welcome speech (either by the couple, or by a parent or friend) no other speeches are really needed. Many couples want the night to be about dancing and mingling, not stories and testimonials. Have your maid of honor, best man, and parents give speeches at the rehearsal dinner instead, and spend more time on the dance floor at your wedding.

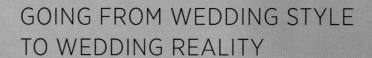

GOING FROM WEDDING STYLE
TO WEDDING REALITY

Every wedding is made up of hundreds of little details. Whether you're single-handedly planning your wedding, hiring a wedding planner, or galvanizing your closest friends to help, the following suggestions will ensure your wedding day success.

Get Organized

There are so many important details to keep track of when planning a wedding—being organized is the name of the game. Most couples opt for keeping most of their important wedding information in a spreadsheet or document that can be shared with all of the key players in the planning process (mother of the bride, groom, wedding planner, etc.). Keep track of the guest list, invoices, checklists, and vendor contracts in one online location so you can easily find what you need.

Create Inspiration Boards

Once you have a wedding style in mind you can look for images to support your vision. Having an inspiration board will be key when explaining your desired look to vendors. Pinterest is a popular way to save your ideas from a variety of online sources in one central location and one that can be easily shared with bridesmaids and vendors. But before you dive into this task, be sure to read my forewarning on page 34.

Look Back On Past Wedding Experiences

Take a few moments to think back on all of the weddings you have attended or played a role in. Make a list of what you liked about them and what you did not. Often times we focus on what we want our wedding to be but forget to think about what we *don't* want it to be. Having past wedding experiences in mind as you plan will help you find a balance between what is a dream wedding and what is reality.

Research Vendors

All good weddings are created with the help of amazing professional vendors. Making a list of potential vendors and reaching out to them will get the ball rolling on who you'll consider working with and if their ideas, prices, and availability match yours.

Put A Planning Timeline Together

Just as every wedding is different so is every timeline. While some couples leave themselves a year or more to plan, others only have a few months. Creating your own timeline will help you nail down what needs to happen and when. Craft your timeline and then decide what the most time-sensitive detail is. Tackling the items that need to happen first might help you to relax on other details, and affords you the ability to focus on one task at a time. Turn the page for a suggested wedding planning timeline.

"I am so visual so I relied heavily on Instagram and Pinterest. The two platforms really allowed me to quickly curate specific looks and themes from which to draw inspiration. More than one element of my wedding day, my bridal shower, and my bachelorette was inspired by those apps!"

—Rachel (Bride)

A WEDDING TIMELINE

When it comes to creating a timeline for your wedding, the best thing you can do is build in extra time. Whether you have six months or eighteen months to plan, try to tackle as much as possible in the earlier phases so you won't be as stressed when you get close to your wedding day.

Here is a sample of a timeline for a twelve-month engagement. Make it your own by adding and subtracting where you see fit.

SUGGESTED WEDDING TIMELINE

12 MONTHS

Select your wedding party

Determine a budget

Make a guest list

Book a venue

Shop for dresses and possibly order

Hire a wedding coordinator or planner

9 MONTHS

Send out save-the-dates

Hire a wedding photographer and videographer

Book your caterer

Set up your wedding registry

Book your band or DJ

6 MONTHS

Book the honeymoon

Order invitations

Purchase wedding rings

Book the florist

Book the rehearsal dinner location

Book your ceremony officiant

Request a room block at hotels near the wedding

3 MONTHS

Order wedding cake or desserts

Order favors and decor items

Book hair and makeup appointments

Send out invitations

1 MONTH OR LESS

Follow up with guests who haven't met your RSVP deadline

Finalize the seating chart

Book a hair and makeup trial appointment

Secure your marriage license

FINDING YOUR STYLE

Boho, rustic, modern, minimalist, romantic, classic...
these are all wedding styles that might work for your
big day. When first developing your wedding style it is
best to stay away from popular social media sites and
wedding blogs *until* you have a defined idea about
what your wedding day should look like.

It is too easy to become inundated, and consequently overwhelmed, with ideas
and styles when browsing online. Instead, begin by coming up with a list of
words to define your big day which remain true to who you and your fiancé are
as a couple. From there, slowly add images to your descriptions. On the next few
pages there are a variety of wedding styles described and suggestions for how
you can achieve their look in a cohesive way.

MODERN

INSPIRATION WORDS
Contemporary, clean, sophisticated

VENUE
Art gallery

FLOWERS
Cream gardenia bouquet

COLOR COMBO
Gold and white

DRESS STYLE
Jumpsuit or structured off-the-shoulder dress

UNIQUE DETAIL
A leather jacket worn over the wedding dress

HONEYMOON
Morocco

STARTER
Tomatoes, Right Now, From the Farm
Kutchkie Peppers & Chiles, Tomato
Water, Basil Oil, Herbs & Blossoms

ENTRÉES
Black Trumpet Crusted Chicken Breast
Shishito Peppers & Fava Beans,
Sauteed Mushrooms, Charred Corn &
Grilled Tomato Ranchera

Vegetable Ash Crusted Fillet
Ratatouille, Twice Baked Spinach
Mashed Potato & Natural Beef Jus

Vegetarian Option Available Upon Request

DESSERT
Mini Seasonal Pies,
Wedding Cake, Coffee & Tea

MENU

BOHO

INSPIRATION WORDS
Unconventional, unique, offbeat

VENUE
Ranch

FLOWERS
A lush red peony bouquet with pink accents

COLOR COMBO
Red and pink

DRESS STYLE
A backless lace gown with flutter sleeves

UNIQUE DETAIL
Flower crown for the bride and bridesmaids

HONEYMOON
Croatia

RUSTIC

INSPIRATION WORDS
Outdoors, natural beauty, unpretentious

VENUE
Farm or barn

FLOWERS
A vibrant bouquet of dahlias and foliage

COLOR COMBO
Cream and green

UNIQUE DETAIL
Arrive by vintage pickup truck to the reception

HONEYMOON
National park

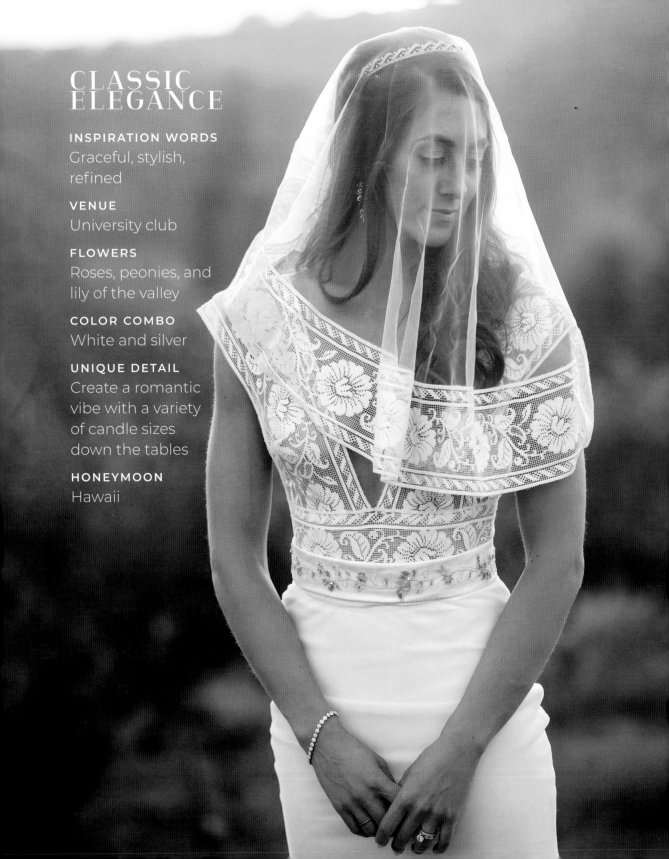

CLASSIC ELEGANCE

INSPIRATION WORDS
Graceful, stylish, refined

VENUE
University club

FLOWERS
Roses, peonies, and lily of the valley

COLOR COMBO
White and silver

UNIQUE DETAIL
Create a romantic vibe with a variety of candle sizes down the tables

HONEYMOON
Hawaii

ROMANTIC

INSPIRATION WORDS
Dreamy, fairy-tale, idyllic

VENUE
Outdoor garden

FLOWERS
Neutral bridal bouquet with peonies, astilbe, and lisianthus

COLOR COMBO
Jewel tones

UNIQUE DETAIL
Lantern-lined walkways

HONEYMOON
Nice, France

MINIMALIST

INSPIRATION WORDS
Simplicity, clean lines, understated

VENUE
Factory or loft space

FLOWERS
A small bouquet of roses

COLOR COMBO
White and black

UNIQUE DETAIL
Marble decorated place cards

HONEYMOON
Amalfi Coast, Italy

COUNTRY

INSPIRATION WORDS
Charming, open space,
down-home

VENUE
Vineyard

FLOWERS
A full bouquet of roses
and anemones

COLOR COMBO
Peach and sage

UNIQUE DETAIL
Mason jar drinks

HONEYMOON
Sonoma, California

METROPOLITAN

INSPIRATION WORDS
Cosmopolitan, urban chic, fashionable

VENUE
Museum or library

FLOWERS
White peony and garden rose bouquet

COLOR COMBO
Pink and gray

UNIQUE DETAIL
Take a classic yellow cab from the ceremony to reception

HONEYMOON
Paris, France

5 QUESTIONS TO ASK WHEN SELECTING A STYLE

1. Does my venue support my intended style?

2. Can I achieve my desired look with my budget?

3. Are there cultural elements I want to include in the look?

4. Do I want my theme to be very specific or a loose interpretation?

5. Will the season play a part in my wedding style?

Say "YES" when people ask if there's anything they can do to help. You're not inconveniencing them. They actually want to help. Let them help.

—Kerry (Bride)

Can I have more than one style I am working with?

Yes! Without question, you are invited to blend together more than one style to create your dream wedding day. I have heard many couples say they want a bohemian event in a rustic setting, or they want classic elegance with a modern edge. The key when working with more than one style is to be specific about what it is you particularly like about each style. This will allow for the styles to be pulled together like carefully curated puzzle pieces rather than a contradictory mess. Adding a modern edge to your event might mean using long wooden tables without table coverings or using bistro-style chairs instead of the traditional "wedding chair." Or mix romance into a modern celebration by using marble plate chargers on a table lined with white candles in unique geometric candle holders.

"We wanted our wedding day to reflect us and how people know us. We are relaxed, and love the outdoors and the rustic romantic look, so we combined beautiful wood slices, peonies, fairy lights, and blue accents into our decor. It was the perfect combination."

—Francine (Bride)

What if I want a specific style but I have limited venue options?

This "problem" is actually more common than not. Most couples are offered only the venues in the area surrounding where they live so it is possible their venue will not fit their specific style. If you happen to fall into this category, fear not. Your dream wedding day can still be brought to life. A wedding style is in the details and the decor. Add perfectly placed decorations with thoughtful details and your venue will become your perfect location.

How can I work my specific style into all the parts of the wedding?

Look at your big budget items like flowers, dress, food, and venue. It is in those areas that you will be able to work your specific style into the wedding. Naturally the venue you book will represent a specific look as will the flowers you choose to carry and decorate with. Selecting food choices that carry out your theme (such as offering food trucks at a backyard wedding or high-end pizza served at an outdoor function) lets your style shine. Once you have nailed down the look for these larger budget items you can then start to work on bringing your unique look to the details such as candles, table decorations and linens, and rental items like plates and glassware choices.

I have always loved the classic, simple sophistication of black and gold. Our venue was decorated for the winter holidays with dozens of trees and white lights which were the perfect backdrop for the color palette we chose: subdued creams and golds with accents of black.

—**Rachel** (Bride)

INVITATIONS, PAPER & STATIONERY

Receiving a wedding invitation in the mail is a wonderful feeling, a feeling of being wanted by a couple to be witness to the most joyous celebration of love. Save-the-dates, invitations, and the stationery that goes along with the wedding celebration are little snippets into what type of day the guests will be participating in. A phrase like *black tie*, images of a canoe and lake, or destination wedding information all allow the guests to prepare for what type of day they will attend.

EPLY

kindly respond by August 26

YES | NO

MR. AND MRS. BOB PEABODY

99999 South Apt. 99
New York, New York 10000

tions;

BEEF

DEPALO/FRANCIA

122456 Park Avenue Apartment 999
New York, New York 10000

it our website for details

EANDTEDDY.COM

STATIONERY PRODUCTS

Save-the-date cards	RSVP cards
Invitations	Reception cards
Rehearsal dinner invitation	Accommodation and travel cards
Menu cards	Table numbers
Ceremony programs	Favor tags
Thank you cards	Place cards

What is a wedding stationery suite?

The term "stationery suite" simply refers to the entire collection of wedding paper sent to the guests, including the save-the-date, invitation, RSVP card, and any other paper you wish to add such as direction cards, accommodation cards, etc.

5 PLACES TO FIND INSPIRATION
FOR YOUR WEDDING STATIONERY

1. Wedding location attractions and postcards

Spend some time digging into the location of where your wedding will take place. You might be lucky enough to find a symbol or saying that you want to include in your stationery suite. A quick online search of vintage postcards from the location can also add to the inspiration.

2. Wallpaper

From florals to stripes, wallpaper can be the ultimate source of inspiration for wedding invitations.

3. Fabric and textiles

Think tablecloths, vintage dresses, lace from your mother's wedding dress or ribbon—even the smallest piece of fabric can help create an entire stationery suite.

4. Your parents' wedding invitations

Pull your parents or grandparents wedding invitations out and study them closely. You might fall in love with the font, paper texture, or design.

5. Vintage magazines and books

Look at the colors, design layout, and paper style and you will find something that inspires you without question.

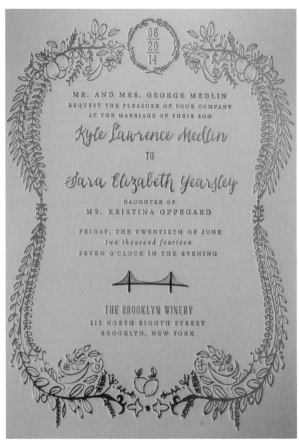

Can I save money and just use email invites?

With the overwhelming amount of emails we receive each day it seems all too likely your important wedding invitation could slip past your guests. There are so many options available for paper invitations and sources to fit every budget, I strongly encourage you to send a paper invitation, even if it's a simple post card.

Can I skip the save-the-date and just send out an invitation?

Yes, you can skip the save-the-date. However, it is always best to give your guests ample time to plan for your wedding—sending out a save-the-date is a courtesy. If you want to skip it (either for budget reasons or you feel they are too formal), at least send out an online option or a simple email so your guests will feel informed about the important date and can start to plan for travel and accommodations.

How can I nicely say no children are invited to our wedding?

There are some pretty good options for letting your guests know you are aiming for an adults-only reception. One of the easiest ways to communicate this idea is to address the invitation to "Mr. & Mrs. Invited Guest," leaving off the wording "and family" or "and children." Even though that should do the trick, you can't always assume everyone is up on their wedding invitation etiquette so you might need to be more direct. If you are including a reception card with the invitation (a separate piece of stationery with the information about where and when the reception will be held), it is perfectly acceptable to add wording such as "Adult reception immediately following ceremony."

DRESSES & ATTIRE

Some dream about the way they will look on their wedding day for years and others only start to think about it once they have said yes to the proposal. No matter which category you fall in, there is a wedding look and style that is perfect for you.

Wedding dress shopping can be overwhelming, especially with all of the content and sources available online and in print to inspire your look. To help you stay focused and enjoy wedding dress shopping, this chapter covers the essential things to keep in mind.

Start shopping early
When it comes to dress shopping, the earlier the better. You want to give yourself time to find the perfect dress, and have it ordered and tailored.

Bring only a select group of people
Resist the urge to bring all your friends, family, and bridesmaids. Having too large of a group opens the door to lots of different opinions and that can be overwhelming. Having just a few important people in your life shop with you can make it meaningful, fun, and stress free.

Keep a budget in mind
You might not stick to your budget but it is best to always have an idea in mind when you start to shop. Avoid sticker shock and do your research on designers so you know if you are looking at one thousand dollar dresses or ten thousand dollar dresses.

Be open to new looks and styles
I once heard you should not say no to a dress until it's zipped and cinched, meaning: try it on and you might be surprised. Also, many styles can be altered so don't say no too early to a dress with or without straps since those details can be changed to fit your look.

Keep your wedding date, location, and weather in mind
Taking your wedding season, location, and possible weather into consideration is key when selecting a dress because it means you will be considering proper fabric and dress styles. Talk with your bridal shop about where and when the wedding is so they can help guide you.

Bring shoes
I know it might seem difficult to bring shoes since you don't know what style dress you will be wearing but bringing your own high heels (especially ones already broken in) will make you feel much more comfortable trying on and walking around in potential wedding dresses. You don't need the exact shoes you will be wearing until you get to the fitting stage of the game but if you know you want to rock flats, sneakers, or sandals on your wedding day then make sure to bring something similar when trying on dresses.

Find unique inspiration
Thanks to online tools like Instagram, Pinterest, and wedding sources like RusticWeddingChic.com, brides can find wedding dress styles in seconds, but think about other inspiration for your wedding day. Consider a red carpet look from a celebrity, your mother or grandmother's wedding dress, or a dress you already own that you love the fit of.

Know the dress lingo
There is an entire wedding dress language and it's important that you get familiar with the terms before you head into your shopping experience. Terms like A-line, sweetheart neckline, and cathedral length are just a few of the terms you should be familiar with. A simple online search will help you get schooled in this new language which you'll find helpful to know.

Understand it is a process
Walking into your first bridal dress appointment and walking out with the perfect dress might happen, but more often than not it doesn't. You might have to try on many more dresses and shop at several different locations before you find the outfit that makes you feel perfect. Accepting that dress shopping might be a longer process than you'd originally expected allows you to move through the process without the stress.

Get all the costs up front
When you plan a wedding you know you will be dealing with big cost, but no one ever wants to be surprised by smaller, add-on costs. When purchasing your dress get all the costs you will be responsible for with the dress in writing. Make sure you confirm what the cost will be for things such as shipping, alterations, cleaning, and extra material if needed.

TIMELESS TRADITION
A clean and classic look that lends itself to an elegant ball gown–style dress

ROMANCE
Think off-the-shoulder straps and long, flowy silhouettes to create a dreamy look

RUSTIC
Classic-meets-country with the option to add rustic accessories like cowboy boots or a gingham ribbon

VINTAGE
Lots of lace with stunning necklines and long veils

BOHO
A smocked bodice and layers of Mexican-style lace are a must

MODERN
A clean and sculpted look lends itself to the modern style

CITY HALL BRIDE
Short or long are both options but so is a jumpsuit!

CASUAL AND DESTINATION
A fitted dress in lovely silk always works

GLAMOUR
Create an old-Hollywood look with satin and covered buttons

COLOR CRAZY
For the bride not afraid of shaking off tradition and adding her own signature color to the day

There are thousands of combinations when it comes to wedding day looks but the following pages include a few of the most popular styles and how you can bring them to life.

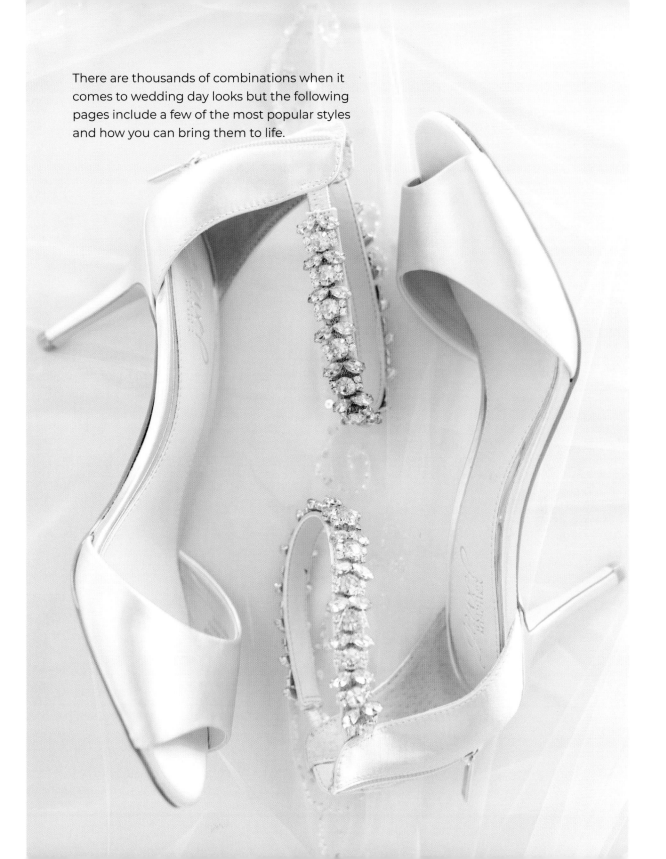

From black tie formal to boho beachy, brides are creating a wedding day look that is 100 percent unique and a reflection of their own personal style. Given the amount of online resources and large number of wedding dress retailers it is not surprising that brides are crafting their own look and not simply selecting a standard all-white gown. Take time to reflect on how you can best make your personal style shine on your wedding day.

"When it was time to pick out my wedding dress, I realized I didn't want to wear a white dress. I love colors and details that I couldn't find in a traditional wedding dress. I chose to wear a dress that was cream and dusty rose with vintage beading. Since blue is my husband's favorite color, we decided blues would go nicely with the color scheme. The bridesmaids wore sapphire blue dresses and the groom and groomsmen wore grays and blues."

—Francine (Bride)

MAGGIE'S TIP: *Pack a pair of flats or sandals and stash them close to the dance floor so you can change as your reception goes on. You might find your feet start to get fatigued after sporting your heels for hours!*

5 WAYS TO MAKE YOUR WEDDING LOOK ALL YOUR OWN

1. Denim jacket

Not just for the country or rustic bride anymore, many modern brides are adding a denim jacket (especially a cropped one) to their ensemble as the evening goes on. One fun idea is having the jacket personalized for the big day to sport your new monogram or your wedding date.

2. Wrap or blanket

This idea has been making brides and bridesmaid happy and warm for a long time but more recently brides have been selecting oversized wraps in fun patterns like buffalo plaids, geometric designs, or preppy stripes to further personalize the look.

3. Leather jacket

The coolest of the cool add a leather jacket to their wedding day attire. Bright white leather, metallic, or jet black—the leather jacket is one we cannot get enough of on brides (and grooms).

4. Color heels or shoes

Brides have been mixing it up when it comes to footwear for some time now but deciding to walk down the aisle in brightly colored shoes still makes our heart jump! It seems no color is off-limits and brides are sporting everything from colorful high heels to sneakers as one more way to personalize their wedding look.

5. Go Barefoot

Getting back to nature and going barefoot on one's wedding day might not be for everyone but it certainly has a place in the wedding world. Previously it seemed that only beach brides were going with the no-shoes look, but I have seen this crop up in other weddings recently and it seems to be gaining in popularity.

What is the difference between white tie, black tie, and black tie optional?

"White tie" (which sometimes is referred to as "full evening dress") requires the men to wear tuxedos with tails and a white vest. As the most formal of styles, a white tie event calls for ladies to wear a full ball gown, often paired with long gloves.

"Black tie" also signifies that your event is formal and suggests that men wear tuxedos and bow ties and women wear cocktail or evening dresses.

When stating your wedding will be "black tie optional" you are informing the guests that men can wear a tuxedo or a dark suit (implying tuxedos are not required).

If you are thinking about having a white tie, black tie, or black tie optional event, ask yourself if your venue lends itself to the specific dress required. Will your guests be comfortable? You might want a very formal barn wedding, however asking women to wear full-length dresses in a barn is not practical. Taking the venue into consideration is a must!

There are other options outside of black tie; your wedding could be formal or even semi-formal. A formal wedding invites your guests to wear long gowns and allows men to wear a tux but a suit is acceptable as well. Semi-formal is a good option for couples who still want an elevated look at the wedding, but allows a little more flexibility: women can wear a short or long dress and men can wear a suit, jacket, or coat.

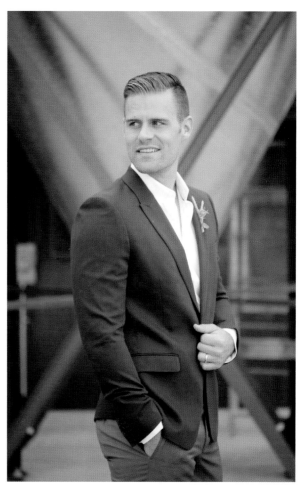

What are some good options for the groom if he is not wearing a tux?

Not every groom wants to rock a classic tuxedo on his wedding day, but not to worry. There are lots of options that will still make your mate look amazing. Many grooms are going with a more casual suit in navy blue, gray, or even tan. Help your groom customize his look by adding details like a gingham print tie for a rustic or country wedding, sneakers for a casual backyard wedding, or a pop of color like a pink shirt for your beachside "I dos."

How can I help my bridesmaids select the perfect dress?

Offering different dress options for your bridesmaids is a wonderful way to make them feel and look great come wedding day. No two bridesmaids are exactly the same so perhaps their dresses don't have to be either. Many dress designers are offering bridesmaid dresses that work together but have slight differences (such as necklines or bodices) so that all women can fit perfectly in their dress. Consider selecting one color and then having your bridesmaids pick out their own dress style. Or think about finding a skirt and top option that would work for everyone. The best way to make your bridesmaids happy is to help them find a dress they feel happy in.

The whole point of picking our own dresses was that the bride wanted us to be comfortable on the big day—and that's exactly what she achieved. It sounds obvious, but open communication, transparency, and a neutral palette were key!

—Katherine (**Maid of Honor**)

How can I mix and match bridesmaid dresses and still have a cohesive look?

The mix and match look is still going strong and is one of my personal favorites! Asking bridesmaids to choose their own dress allows for everyone to feel comfortable on the wedding day. However, many brides struggle with how to create a cohesive look with different dress styles and colors.

One of the best ways to achieve a cohesive look is to work with one color family. You might want to offer your bridesmaids the ability to select any dress style within the gray and charcoal family or any dress in metallics. You might want to give some guidelines such as fabric type, length, and details like beading. This will allow your brides- maids to shop with confidence and for you to feel happy with their dress choice.

The bride asked that we stay within a gold, champagne, or dusty rose color scheme, and wanted to try to vary the level and types of embellishments. But the most important thing to her was that we all found a dress that we felt beautiful in and that felt like "us."

—Katherine (Maid Of Honor)

FLOWERS, BOUQUETS & CENTERPIECES

The flowers you select for your wedding go beyond just another simple detail—they are a statement piece for your celebration. Flowers can take a starring role at your wedding: not only do you walk down the aisle with them, but they can inspire the backdrop for the rest of your decorations. Creating swoon-worthy flowers is often done with the help of a great florist, one that can help you create your vision while keeping in mind the season and your budget. Start gathering ideas early on in the wedding planning process for your flowers and bouquets since many other details can be based on your florals.

5 TECHNIQUES FOR SELECTING YOUR WEDDING FLOWERS

1. Be inspired by others

Start researching online and find a variety of examples you like so you can share some visuals with your florist. Oftentimes what we see online and in magazines are large-budget florals so it is important to ask how you can achieve the look you want on your budget.

2. Use the season

Find a flower you can use in your details

Look closely at your dress or lace. Is there a flower design in it you can use for your bouquet? Or choose a flower you love and have your baker work it in to the details of your wedding cake.

3. Work with a very specific color theme

It is easy to start falling in love with lots of different flowers and styles. Staying within one color theme should prevent you from bouncing all over the place with different looks.

4. Let your venue be an influence

If you are saying "I do" at a rustic vineyard, you will want to consider flowers that match the surroundings. This same theory works for any type of venue. See what is naturally growing (or not) at your venue. You can add to it or let the natural surroundings speak for themselves.

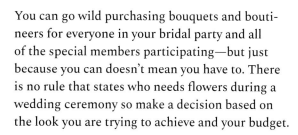

Who should I purchase bouquets for in the wedding party?

You can go wild purchasing bouquets and bouti-neers for everyone in your bridal party and all of the special members participating—but just because you can doesn't mean you have to. There is no rule that states who needs flowers during a wedding ceremony so make a decision based on the look you are trying to achieve and your budget.

I have a large number of tables at the ceremony; do I have to do floral center-pieces on every table?

Large centerpieces on each table can eat up your flower budget quickly. If you have a large wedding guest list you might need to consider a different way of present-ing centerpieces. One foolproof way to save a little is to alternate every other table with a large centerpiece followed at the next table by a smaller one. This will help you create a cohesive look but will save money too. If you are willing to give up the idea of having flowers on every single table you can alternate flowers on one table followed by a non-floral centerpiece on the next.

What are some alternatives to just the classic vase for centerpieces?

The possibilities are endless when it comes to creating alternative containers for your centerpieces and flowers. Birch wrapped vases, wood boxes, colored glass ceramics, and wood or glass bowls are just a few of the many ideas you can use. I love seeing wedding centerpieces in different containers, so think about mixing and matching as well.

FLOWERS FOR ALL LOCATIONS

You know you need to order a bouquet for yourself, and perhaps for your bridesmaids, but you'll probably want to order flowers for several different locations for decor. The following pages contain lists where and for whom you may want to provide flowers. Make sure you create a wish list of all of the florals you would like to have on your wedding day so your florist has a complete list when you have your consultation.

INDIVIDUAL FLORALS

You might have a long list of arrangements you need or a very short one depending on the size of your bridal party and the specific look you are going for.

Bridal bouquet

Bride's hair or floral crown

Bridesmaids bouquets

Groomsmen boutonnieres

Bouquet or corsage for mother of the bride, mother of the groom, grandmothers

Boutonnieres for father of the bride, father of the groom, grandfathers

Flower girl florals

Ring bearer boutonniere

Ushers boutonnieres

Other attendants corsage or boutonniere

Small toss bouquet

CEREMONY

You might be able to repurpose some of these arrangements for your reception. Make sure you discuss this with your florist in order to save a little in your budget. For example, one or two large floral arrangements at the entrance of the ceremony can be repurposed at the entrance of the cocktail hour or the reception space.

Welcome table or entryway

Aisle decorations

Church pews or chair decorations

Alter decorations

Chuppah arrangements

Tossing petals for flower girl

COCKTAIL HOUR & RECEPTION

Flowers are the way most couples decorate their space and of course you'll need more than a few perfectly placed centerpieces. You might want to consider ordering arrangements for the following areas of your reception, but before you do, check in with your venue. Many times they have permanent floral arrangements at the space. You don't want to spend money on something that's already provided.

Escort card table

Main doors or entryway

At the base of tent poles (for a tented reception)

Bride and groom chair decorations

Table centerpieces

Bar, dessert, and food tables

Cake table

Cocktail tables

Bathroom and lounge areas

Getaway car

THE NON-FLORAL CENTERPIECES

Not everyone wants floral arrangements on every table; deciding to go with non-floral centerpieces to make a statement may work for you. Choose objects that complement your theme or make a statement about you and your partner. Here are a few of the best non-floral centerpiece ideas.

Books	Framed pictures	Wheat
Lanterns	Maps and globes	Herbs
Candles	Fruit	Wedding favors
Plants	Sea shells	Pinecones
Vintage cameras	Decorative ornaments	

How much of my budget should I put towards flowers?

It is often calculated that somewhere between eight and ten percent of your overall budget will go toward florals (including bouquets). It is very easy to get carried away when looking at beautiful floral arrangements so if you are trying to stay within a certain budget for flowers be up-front with your florist. Tell them how much you would like to spend and they can help you achieve your desired look.

What if my bouquet does not end up looking like what I had wanted?

This can happen. I know firsthand how disappointing it can be when the flowers arrive on your wedding day and they look different from what you had agreed on with your florist. If your flowers are not up to your specifications you should first talk with the florist. See what they can do in a few hours to get you closer to your dream wedding bouquet. You can also take matters into your hands (only if you are feeling confidant) and make a few changes yourself. On my own wedding day I did not love my bouquet, but I was able to snip a few extra pieces, tighten up the flowers, and rewrap the ribbon around the stems—and ended up with something I was much happier with.

Can I DIY my own wedding flowers?

Since flowers take up such a large part of the budget it seems logical that many couples would want to save a little money and take this task on themselves. Creating your own wedding flowers is a much larger task than you first think. Don't forget that flowers need to stay cool so you must have some way of refrigerating a large quantity of arrangements.

If you are using a small number of bouquets or floral arrangements you can take on DIYing the flowers, but make sure you have a very specific plan of how you will order the flowers, where you will store them, and definitely do a trial run of your most important arrangements a few weeks before the big day.

CEREMONY & VOWS

The ceremony is the moment you have been looking forward to since you said "yes" to the perfect proposal. After careful months of planning and coordinating, you and your fiancé will stand up in front of loved ones and share your vows. Your ceremony should be unique to you and your partner and represent you as a couple. From traditional faith-based services to informal, quick ceremonies, the exchanging of vows is what a wedding is all about.

DOS & DON'TS WHEN PLANNING YOUR CEREMONY

Do: Book your wedding officiant early in the planning process—right after your select your date!

Don't: Select a ceremony location too far from the reception venue. Keeping it under forty-five minutes is ideal for guests

Do: Make sure your ceremony location can comfortably fit your guest list

Don't: Forget about how the weather will impact your ceremony location

Do: Spend some of your budget on decorating the ceremony location

Don't: Expect everyone to have transportation from one location to another. Providing some sort of trolly or bus is always welcome

Do: Provide background and insights about traditions and key people in a wedding program

Don't: Select a large wedding party if your wedding ceremony will be small and intimate

Soak it all up and let your heart be filled over and over again with all the incredible moments that make your wedding day.

—Adessa (Bride)

5 WAYS TO MAKE YOUR CEREMONY TOTALLY UNIQUE

1. **Play music special to you and your partner**

2. **Create a wedding program that is a little funny and upbeat**

3. **Add decor that speaks to your theme and represents your style**

4. **Serve drinks at the ceremony so guests can get festive right away**

5. **Create unique seating: allow guests to surround you in a circle or sit on blankets or benches**

Do I have to have readings and speakers at my wedding ceremony?

A wedding ceremony should be 100 percent exactly how you want it to be. So, no, you don't need to have certain readings or speakers at your ceremony. Instead of readings you should think of creative ways to share some important messages, such as playing a meaningful song or asking your guests to all read a short poem together out loud.

How can I make sure my ceremony does not go longer than forty-five minutes or so?

The main reason everyone is in attendance is to watch you say your vows so make sure you don't plan a ceremony that is *too* short. If you are set on having a ceremony under a specific length of time, communication is key. Make sure your officiant knows you would like a shorter ceremony; this way they can plan how much speaking they will do. Cutting down on readings and having a small bridal party will help shorten the ceremony length as well. You can also limit how much music is played. If your ceremony is faith-based, talk with your officiant to see which part of the service you can skip.

RECEPTION, DECOR & MORE

You said "I do" and now it is time to celebrate! For many couples the reception is the time when they can relax and really have fun. Just as each couple is unique, so is their wedding reception. There really is no cookie-cutter wedding reception anymore. From large lavish ballrooms to refurbished historic barns, creating a look and style for your reception goes beyond the venue. Think: festive food, creative decorations, and totally unique spins on tradition.

MAGGIE'S TIP: *Skip the champagne toast and allow guests to cheer you with whatever they are drinking. At least make sure your catering company asks if your guests would like a glass of champagne so you don't have a lot of unwanted champagne flutes sitting around.*

CREATIVE RECEPTION IDEAS

Use square or long tables to create a different seating vibe

Host a lounge area close to the bar area so people can grab a drink and sit comfortably

Organize a kids station filled with games and crafts

Hand out late-night snacks to go

Offer flip-flops for dancing shoes

Set out lawn games

Arrange for food trucks to serve food

Ditch the head table and sit at a sweethearts table

Hand out cozy blankets at a fall or winter wedding

Personalize your cocktail napkins with fun sayings

Rent benches or mismatched chairs for an eclectic look

Create a unique guest book by using a paddle, map, sign, or piece of wood

How can I personalize my venue and make it look unique?

Start with a few big details like floral arrangements, table coverings, and the type of furniture you want to see at your event. If you want to bring in rented items for a lounge area you can customize it to look like any style from vintage to modern. Floral arrangements can also have a big impact on how the venue space looks so talk with your florist about adding a few "wow" pieces, such as large arrangements for the entryway, arches, or even hanging flowers. Don't be afraid to work with color. Many couples think of white as a traditional wedding color and shy away from adding pops of color to their space. A little (or a lot of) color can really make the space unique to your vision. Don't feel boxed into a one-color wedding linen. I have seen plaids, stripes, patterned, polka dot, and even textured linens. Don't forget to ask about coverings like long table runners instead of the traditional table cover, and think about mixing and matching two or even three different types of coverings at your reception.

DECOR DETAILS

Oftentimes the reception area is a large blank space that needs lots of love and attention to make it your wedding dream. With such a blank slate it can feel overwhelming to know what to decorate, how to decorate it, and where to skip the decorations. The rest of this chapter is filled with inspiration for finding the right details for your reception space.

TABLES & CHAIRS

Once you know if you are using round, square, or rectangular tables you can focus on the details like which linens you want to have on each table. Think about selecting a table covering that has some texture or going with coverings that all work in the same color family. No one says you need to play it safe and go with just white! If you are going with long, rectangular tables consider using table runners. They can be a less expensive option and add a great pop of color to the table. If you can find room in the budget, ask your venue or rental company for options with chair styles. I have seen everything from clear plastic chairs to natural wood chairs, which adds a little something to the overall look of your venue. Talk with your florist about adding swags of flowers or greenery to chairs as well.

LIGHTING & DRAPERY

You want a romantic mood and nothing can achieve that more easily than adding great lighting. Many venues have a lighting team they can call in to help you achieve your desired ambience. Some couples want a pop of color and some uplighting while others only want small white lights and perfectly placed candles. Whatever your lighting style may be, you should try to see the venue with the lighting you want before the big day if possible. Another way to dress up your reception space is with drapery. Think: long, flowing, white drapes or blush-toned drapery hanging from the ceiling. Working with drapes within your wedding colors can transform your space in no time.

SIGNAGE, TABLE NUMBERS & ESCORT CARDS

Your guests all need to know where to go and where to sit, so spend some time thinking about how you will inform them of these things. There are a lot of good resources online for finding a graphic artist or handletterer to create signage that perfectly fits your style. Signage can be used to communicate to your guests things like cocktails served at the bar, the evening's menu, their seating location, or simply the order of events of the day. For table numbers, begin by checking out the online marketplace Etsy, where you can discover thousands of handmade goods and artists. Couples and event teams have been increasingly creative when thinking of unique ways to display table numbers; we have come a long way from the frame with a number image displayed! There is no limit to how you can showcase your table numbers, escort cards, menus, and more.

159

What is the difference between place cards and escort cards?

An escort card informs the guests which table they will be sitting at, where place cards actually tell guests which seat at the table they will be sitting in. Some couples just offer escort cards while others have both escort and place cards. If you are hosting an extremely formal event you will want to offer both, but this can sometimes be hard to manage, and isn't always necessary.

CREATIVE TABLE NUMBER IDEAS

Wine bottles

Chalkboards

Rocks

Painted glassware

Buoys

Location names & destinations

Maps

Photo numbers

Moss numbers

Agate

Driftwood

Planted table numbers

Wood squares

CREATIVE ESCORT CARD IDEAS

Mini champagne bottles

Sea shells

Leaves

Arrows

Feathers

Chart with flowers or greenery

Fruit or seasonal item like mini pumpkins

Photos of the individual, perhaps with
one or both of the newlyweds

Luggage tags

Pine pillow

BACKDROPS

A perfectly placed backdrop can add some drama behind the head table, or at least behind the bride and groom chairs. If that is not what you have been envisioning, you could add a backdrop behind the bar area, food station, cake display, escort card location, or photo booth! You might have already thought of a backdrop for your ceremony location and you might be able to reuse it at the reception space.

DISHES & DINNERWARE

Throw out all of your preconceived ideas that your reception dinnerware needs to be simple and white. Couples today are finding interesting vendors that specialize in vintage china, modern styles, patterned dishes, and even clear glass—all of which can add your own stamp to your reception tables. When you think about the table settings, you need to factor in glasses and barware as well. Just as we are seeing new trends with dishes, we are seeing them with glassware as well. Everything is in play from stemless champagne flutes to colored glass to copper mugs for speciality drinks.

FESTIVE FOOD

A main focus of your reception and one of the easiest ways to put a personal spin on your day is the food, so don't settle for run-of-the-mill catering options. Start researching catering companies early so you can get a chance to meet with a few before making your decision. If your venue also provides a catering team, consider asking if (in addition to the meal they'll be serving) you can bring in another vendor for specific, more festive food options.

As the event goes on and the dancing is starting to heat up, think about offering guests a late-night snack. Not only will this make your guests' tummies happy but it can also be a good way to wind down the bar service and say good night.

5 LATE NIGHT FOOD OPTIONS YOU CAN SERVE

1. Pizza slices
2. Mini tacos
3. Bite-size sandwiches
4. Grilled cheese alongside soup in a shot glass
5. Cookie with a mini carton of milk

MAGGIE'S TIP: *A coffee bar is a great way to allow your guests to grab a little cup of caffeine as the night winds down. This can be a great way to signal the last hour of your reception by segueing from an alcohol bar to a coffee bar.*

CAKES, DESSERTS & TREATS

Since I launched RusticWeddingChic.com in 2008,
it seems like a million different dessert trends have
emerged onto the wedding scene. From country
pies to cupcakes to s'mores, couples are serving up
after-dinner sweets in a variety of styles. The dessert
table and cake design is a place where couples can
add a little more fun into their day. I always love how
inventive couples are with their cake design and
how creative they are with their wedding desserts.
The following pages highlight a number of the
best cake trends to suit every wedding style.

THE PETITE CAKE

A small wedding cake usually made up of only one layer which can be decorated as elaborately or as understated as you see fit. Oftentimes couples will serve several petite cakes either all in the same style or in a variety of designs or flavors. This is a great option when you don't want to choose just one kind of cake!

THE NAKED CAKE

A wedding cake that is void (or offers a limited outer layer) of frosting. Some naked cakes have no frosting at all on the outside while others have just a small amount for decoration.

THE ALL-WHITE CAKE

Still a popular option is the all-white wedding cake. Complete with decorations like flowers or ribbons of frosting, the all-white wedding cake can be as dressed up or dressed down as you like to fit your theme and style.

THE FRUIT CAKE

Fruit has made an amazing comeback as a popular wedding cake design in the last few years. From country-inspired styles to rustic chic ones, a fruit cake allows couples to go with a more natural design and taste. If you are thinking of serving a fruit cake, try to find a bakery that will work with a local source so you can serve local fruit to your guests.

THE COLOR CAKE

Gone are the days when every item at a wedding needs to be white. Couples who are looking to make a big impact often decide to spice up their wedding cake with bright colors.

THE TRADITIONAL TIERED CAKE

Traditional in size but not in style. Many couples might choose to have a cake upward of four layers but that does not mean they are settling for a boring design.

MORE CAKE DESIGNS WORTH CHECKING OUT

Metallic

Art deco

Painted cake

Modern geometric

Textured buttercream

Geode cake

Dark cake

MAGGIE'S TIP: *Many of the guests will be busy dancing, mingling, and enjoying the reception—not just sitting at their table. Ask your catering staff not to cut the cake and place it at each seat (this often results in lots of uneaten cake). Instead ask the staff to place the cake in one central location so guests who are interested can come up and take a piece when they are ready.*

Can I still serve the traditional wedding cake?

Of course! There is nothing that says you need to move with the trends and go for a more modern dessert. If you have always dreamed of having a traditional multi-layer wedding cake, then go for it!

Why do couples order a wedding cake and *a groom's cake*?

Traditionally, a couple orders a wedding cake that they cut and then serve to the wedding guests. In addition, many couples order a groom's cake which is normally decorated in a way that reflects the groom's interests, hobbies, or passions. Many times a groom will choose a cake that reflects his style and frankly, it is just a fun way to allow your groom to have a wedding detail that is all about him.

How can I serve different options for dessert?

I know many brides who would like to have a traditional wedding cake (and a cake-cutting photo) but also want to wow their guests with some additions to the dessert menu. If you are thinking you would like to do something like this, start by talking with your catering company or bakery who will be supplying the cake and see what options could be a good a match. Guests love to grab a sweet treat as they dance or mingle so having a dessert station in addition to the cake served is a great way to allow your guests to indulge. I have seen everything from a cookie station to a popcorn buffet to a trail mix bar—get creative and have fun.

5 COMPLETELY DIFFERENT DESSERT IDEAS

Donut wall
How and why this became so popular so fast can only be attributed to social media but we are so thankful this idea has made the rounds. Setting up a donut wall or location is now easier than ever since so many gourmet donut companies have popped up in recent years leading to inventive and wild flavors.

Candy buffet
The wedding candy buffet will bring out the child in all of your guests allowing them to mix and match flavors of the candies they love. Go beyond offering a simple paper bag and think about fun containers such as clear plastic boxes, metal tins, mini tote bags, or mason jars for your guests to take home their loot. Think about arranging your candy buffet by color and then mix and match different containers for different candies, making the display look like a wonderful mini candy shop.

Ice cream sundae station
No one turns down a good ice cream sundae station! You can either research ice cream trucks that will set this up for you at your reception, or work with your catering team to scoop ice cream and then allow your guests to complete their creation with a variety of toppings!

Cookie bar
Not only is the cookie bar a budget saving trick but it is also fun to create. Display a large array of cookie flavors in different ways using various displays. Offer guests a monogrammed (or otherwise personalized) paper bag to take home their treat. A fun addition to this idea is to offer cookies with meaning to you, such as the groom's mother's famous oatmeal cookie or your grandma's chocolate chip cookie.

Cupcake tower
Although this idea is not exactly new it is always a crowd pleaser. Think about selecting smaller cupcakes so no forks or plates are needed. Guests can grab a cupcake and head back to the dance floor! Some of the most successful cupcake towers I have seen offer a variety of flavors ensuring all guests are happy.

FAVORS

Traditionally the wedding couple offers a small token of appreciation to their guests by handing out a wedding favor. There are so many creative options available—the possibilities are endless for what type of favor you can give.

WEDDING FAVOR IDEAS

Cookies

Jams & jellies

Mini bottles of champagne

Candles

Soap

Trail mix

Shot glasses

Candy

Fresh produce from a mini farm stand

MAGGIE'S TIP: *Buying umbrellas to have on hand is never a bad idea. Even if your ceremony or reception is not outside, your guests going from the car to your reception location will be happier dry and not wet! If you don't use them, great. This is probably an item you can return if unused.*

SEND-OFFS, HONEYMOONS & HAPPILY EVER AFTERS

As you and your partner plan your send off (whether you're headed home to crash for the night, being whisked off in a cab to a hotel, or hightailing it to catch your red-eye honeymoon flight), keep in mind that the wedding day farewells and the thank-you hugs may become some of your sweetest memories of the whole celebration. It's a moment to step back and take in a scene brimming with friends and family who've gathered with the sole purpose of celebrating the two of you. It's a powerful moment! Revel in it. Plan this portion of the festivities with as much personal flair and attention as you give the ceremony and reception. The end of your wedding day is just the beginning of your marriage— make every moment as unique as you are.

SEND-OFFS

After the vows, dinner, dancing, and cake, it is time to say goodbye to your guests.

Marking the end of the wedding reception and leaving your venue with a celebratory send-off is the perfect way to mark the passage from wedding to honeymoon. Couples often ask their guests to line up and see them off as the evening comes to an end. To add a little extra festivity to the moment supply your guests with something they can shower you with as you exit. Working with your event team and the venue so all of the items are in place will ensure that you have a successful send-off.

SEND-OFF SUGGESTIONS

Glitter

Sparklers

Bubbles

Colorful pom-poms

Flower petals

Streamers

Sky lanterns

Confetti

Glow sticks

Fireworks

GETAWAY VEHICLES

Leaving your wedding reception should be one last way to celebrate your new status as a married couple. Many couples are moving away from the typical limo and driving away in style. Consider having one of the following getaway vehicles to end your big day.

Vintage car	**Motor scooter**
Pickup truck	**Bike**
Boat	**Classic yellow taxi**
Golf cart	**Trolley**

?

What are some ways I can decorate my getaway car?

Depending on what type of getaway vehicle you choose for your big day there are so many fun options on how to decorate it. Some couples decide to stay with an elegant look and decorate with flowers or a swag of greenery while some couples go the more playful route and add streamers, signs, bows and even the classic tin cans tied to string. Whatever look you decide to go with make sure you have it listed as a line item in your budget; this fun detail is often be overlooked.

HONEYMOON MUST-HAVES

A honeymoon is your chance to rest, relax, and recover after your amazing wedding day. The months leading up to the big day can be stressful and of course the wedding day can be long. Taking a honeymoon is your chance to reconnect as a couple and enjoy some downtime.

Should we take a honeymoon right after the wedding or wait?

This is up to you and your partner. Traditionally, couples took a honeymoon right after the wedding as a way to relax from the stress of the wedding planning and wedding day itself. It's a special way to keep the romance of the wedding festivities going; after the thrill of a full weekend celebrating with your dearest family and friends, most newlyweds would be reluctant to return to their desk the following Monday.

Although it is still popular to leave for the honeymoon post-wedding, many couples decide to wait for a variety of reasons. Some couples have to fit their honeymoon into their work vacation times while others want to save up some additional funds. If you're unable to get away for the honeymoon of your dreams right after the wedding, consider a "mini-moon." A mini-moon has become a popular option for couples who either need a little more time to save for their honeymoon after their big day or are just opting to take their honeymoon at a later time. No matter when you decide to go on a honeymoon, it is important to take some time for you and your partner to get away, connect, and enjoy being a married couple.

What are some alternatives to your typical resort honeymoon?

If the idea of sitting by a pool at a resort is not your ideal honeymoon, that is perfectly okay. Skipping the resort-style hotel means you'll have to plan more details yourself but with a little extra time and research, you and your partner will be able to craft the honeymoon experience you've always dreamed of.

Check out options for a vacation rental house or a boutique hotel in the places that pique your interest. Is your favorite band on tour in a city you'd like to visit? Plan your honeymoon around the concert you know you and your new spouse will love. Festivals are also a great option; whether you're into beer, indie films, theater, art, technology, Wicca, or Eeyore (yes, *that* Eeyore), there is a festival for you. Or think of a location in a mutual favorite book or film that you've always wanted to visit. Maybe you'll end up in New York, retracing the steps of Jay Gatsby or Holden Caulfield; or in England, reminiscing about your favorite scenes from *Pride & Prejudice* or *Harry Potter*. You can visit the Ernest Hemingway House in Cuba or John Steinbeck's childhood home near Monterey, California. Perhaps you've always dreamed of a tropical destination wedding but, due to budget constraints or family members unable to travel, couldn't make it work—take your honeymoon there instead! Lastly, who says you have to go somewhere new? Book a trip to your favorite get-away and enjoy taking in the familiar haunts with your newlywed eyes.

There are so many options out there. Find the one that will allow you to have a honeymoon that fits your style.

RESOURCES

PHOTOGRAPHERS

Anée Atelier
Pages 48, 49, 50, 51, 73, 79, 94, 162, 164
Aneeatelier.com

Ava Moore Photography
Pages 20 (right), 44, 45, 46, 47, 115 (right), 124, 136, 172
avamoorephotography.com

Bakerture Photography and Video
Page 127 (bottom)
bakerture.com

Blue Locket Studios
Pages 20 (left), 28, 115 (left), 151, 178
bluelocket.com

Caitlin Gilbert Photography
Pages 52, 53 (right), 89, 108, 112, 117, 118 (bottom), 126, 148, 156, 170, 176,
caitlingilbertphotography.com

Christine Grace Photography
Pages 6, 24, 71, 76, 81, 86 (right), 96, 110, 121, 128, 134, 152, 153, 161, 168, 174, 183 (right), 184, 187, 190 (top), 201
christinegracephotography.com

Diana Foley Photography
Page 146 (left)
vermontphotography.net

Erin Johnson
Pages 68, 69, 132, 155, 183 (left)
erinjohnsonphoto.com

Gerry Sulp
Pages 22 (top), 25, 26, 29 (top), 40, 41, 42, 43, 60, 61, 62, 63, 92, 93 (top), 138, 141, 173, 177
gerrysulp.net

Josh Goodman Photography
Pages 23, 113, 125, 142, 160 (top), 180, 189, 190 (bottom), 194–195
joshgoodman.com

Lillie Fortino Photography
Pages 30, 31, 80 (left), 91, 100, 120, 133, 146 (right), 150, 175, 179, 185, 193
lilliefortino.com

Logan Cole Photography
Pages 17, 18, 36, 37, 38, 55, 74, 95, 127 (top), 160 (bottom), 181, 196
logancoleblog.com

Loree Photography
Pages 22 (bottom), 105, 106, 129, 158, 165, 188
loreephotography.com

Love in Theory
Pages 10, 12, 14, 27, 29 (bottom), 32, 34, 53 (left), 64, 65, 66, 67, 70, 80 (right), 82, 86 (left), 98, 123, 130, 140, 144, 159 (top), 163, 167, 182, 202, 206
Loveintheory.com

Paolo Ceritano
Pages 15, 16, 84, 85, 90, 109, 199
paoloceritano.com

Pepper Nix Photography
Pages 78, 101, 114, 118 (top), 157
peppernix.com

Ramblefree Photo Co.
Pages 93 (bottom), 119, 135
ramblefree.com

Sophie Mathewson Photography
Pages 8, 56, 57, 58, 59
sophiemathewson.com

Susan Elizabeth Photography
Pages 21, 77, 102, 103, 116, 159 (bottom), 186
susanelizabethweddings.com

EVENT PLANNERS & DESIGNERS

Bella Giornata Events & Design
(bellagiornataevents.com)

Bluebell Events
(Bluebellevents.com)

Lindsay Plank Events
(Lindsayplankevents.com)

Loli Events
(Lolievents.com)

Peachy Keen Event Rentals and Design
(Peachykeeneventrentals.com)

Sarah Jane Events
(Sarahjaneevents.com)

Smells Like Peonies Events
(Smellslikepeoniesevents.com)

Vivince Event Studio
(Vivince.com)

FLORISTS

Decoration Inc.
(Decorationinc.com)

FLWR
(Flwrstudio.com)

Pocket of Posies Floral Design
(Pocketofposies.ca)

Sham's Florist & Gifts
(Shamsflorist.ca)

Sprout Home
(Sprouthome.com)

The Watering Can Flower Market
(Thewateringcan.ca)

Tickled Floral
(Tickledfloral.com)

STATIONERY

Azure Couture Event Stationery
(Helloazure.com)

Basic Invite
(Basicinvite.com)

Cabin Calligraphy
(Cabincalligraphy.com)

Defining Moments Stationery
(Dmstationery.ca)

Graphically Yours
(graphicallyyours-jc.com)

Mint Lavender and Lace
(Facebook.com/mintlavenderandlace)

CAKES & DESSERTS

Bellas On The Bench
(Bellasonthebenchcakery.com)

Kiwi's Cupcakes & Cakes
(Kiwiscupcakes.com)

Moonshine Donuts
(Moonshinedoughnuts.ca)

Nine Cakes
(Ninecakes.com)

Palermo's Custom Cakes and Bakery
(Palermobakery.com)

Sarah Joy Sweets
(Facebook.com/sarahjoysweets)

Sugar Shack Donuts
(Sugarshackdonuts.com)

ACKNOWLEDGMENTS

No one can create a book without help and I consider myself one lucky girl to be surrounded with the most talented and supportive team. This book would not be possible without the guidance and support from everyone at Gibbs Smith Publishing, especially my editor, Katie Killebrew. Thanks to Kristen Elworthy at Seven Hills Communications for always making me a priority. A big thank you is in order to all of the wedding professionals who added their talents to this book. I especially need to thank my family for understanding how much time and effort it takes to turn out a book and for pitching in when needed. To Jon for always supporting every idea I come up with, and to our boys, Jack, Charlie, and William, who are my everything.

ABOUT THE AUTHOR

The founder of the popular online wedding resource RusticWeddingChic.com, Maggie Lord has spent the past ten years creating, inspiring, and sharing wedding knowledge. Maggie is often seen on TV sharing her insider tips for wedding planning along with her insights on how best to be both a parent and an entrepreneur. Maggie has been profiled in such outlets as *Forbes, Success Magazine, Huffington Post, Fast Company, Entrepreneur, Business Insider,* and others. Maggie is the author of five previous books: *Rustic Wedding Chic, Barn Weddings, The Rustic Wedding Handbook, Color Me Married,* and *Welcome To Babyland.* Maggie lives in Connecticut with her husband, Jon, and their three sons, Jack, Charlie, and William.

Photo credit: Maggie Carson Jurow